STEM IN HOCKEY

SportsZone
imprint of Abdo Publishing
bdopublishing.com

BY BRETT S. MARTIN

ABDOPUBLISHING.COM

Published by Abdo Publishing, a division of ABDO, PO Box 398166, Minneapolis, Minnesota 55439.
Copyright © 2018 by Abdo Consulting Group, Inc. International copyrights reserved in all countries.
No part of this book may be reproduced in any form without written permission from the
publisher. SportsZone™ is a trademark and logo of Abdo Publishing.

Printed in the United States of America, North Mankato, Minnesota
102017
012018

THIS BOOK CONTAINS
RECYCLED MATERIALS

Cover Photo: Gene J. Puskar/AP Images
Interior Photos: Steve Roberts/Cal Sport Media/AP Images, 4–5; Lorraine Swanson/Shutterstock
Images, 6–7; Matt Slocum/AP Images, 8; Mark Humphrey/AP Images, 11, 45; Chris Szagola/AP
Images, 12–13; Fred Kfoury III/Icon Sportswire, 15; Chris O'Meara/AP Images, 16; Julie Jacobson/
AP Images, 19; Jeff Vinnick/National Hockey League/Getty Images, 20–21; Tom Mihalek/AP
Images, 22–23; Frederick Breedon/Getty Images Sport/Getty Images, 25; Ted Thai/The LIFE Picture
Collection/Getty Images, 27; G. Flume/Getty Images Sport/Getty Images, 28–29; AP Images, 30–31;
Shutterstock Images, 32, 41; David Stluka/AP Images, 35; Aaron Doster/Cal Sport Media/AP Images,
37; Eric Risberg/AP Images, 38–39

Editor: Arnold Ringstad
Series Designer: Maggie Villaume
Content Consultant: Patricia D. Morrell, Professor, University of Portland, School of Education

PUBLISHER'S CATALOGING-IN-PUBLICATION DATA

Names: Martin, Brett S., author.
Title: STEM in hockey / by Brett S. Martin.
Description: Minneapolis, Minnesota : Abdo Publishing, 2018. | Series: STEM in sports | Includes
       online resources and index.
Identifiers: LCCN 2017946883 | ISBN 9781532113512 (lib.bdg.) | ISBN 9781532152399 (ebook)
Subjects: LCSH: Hockey--Juvenile literature. | Sports sciences--Juvenile literature. | Physics--
       Juvenile literature.
Classification: DDC 796.357--dc23
LC record available at https://lccn.loc.gov/2017946883

TABLE OF CONTENTS

Sidney Crosby helped lead the Pittsburgh Penguins to victory in the 2017 Stanley Cup Finals.

1

STEM ON
THE RINK

It's the deciding game of the Stanley Cup Finals, the championship series of the National Hockey League (NHL). A player takes control of the loose puck. His skates slice smoothly across the rink as he pushes the puck with his high-tech hockey stick. Gentle taps to the puck are enough to keep it under control as it glides across the ice.

The player pulls the stick back, then whacks the puck. The curve of the blade at the end of the

stick lifts the puck off the ice, sending it flying through the air. It sails over the right shoulder of the goalie and goes into the net for a goal. The player's team ends up taking home the Stanley Cup, the oldest trophy in professional sports.

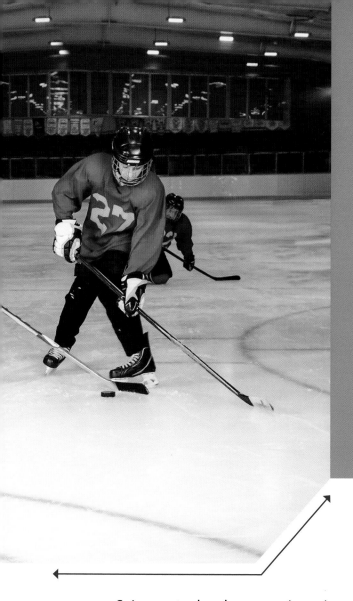

Youth hockey is wildly popular in many parts of the United States.

Science, technology, engineering, and math (STEM) play a big part in hockey. STEM principles help determine the thickness of skate blades and how sharp they should be for the best performance. STEM can predict the direction of a puck after it's shot, allowing

The difference between a save and a goal can be a tiny fraction of a second.

goalies to react quickly enough to make a big save. And all the things a player has when stepping onto the ice, including hockey sticks, skates, protective gear, gloves, and mouth guards, were designed using STEM principles.

ADVANCING THE GAME OF HOCKEY

Hockey is one of the most popular games in the world, with more than 1 million players participating in organized hockey leagues. Being a hockey star requires a broad range of skills and abilities. Players must be expert skaters, and they must also be able to pass and shoot the puck. They need to be strong, too. Some versions of hockey are contact sports. This means players are supposed to body check, or run into the person with the puck. The purpose is to take the puck away, and it requires giving and taking very physical hits using the entire body.

Games are played on an ice rink. Typically, each of the two teams has six players on the ice. A team's six players are split into four positions. There are two defenders, two wings, one center, and a goalie. Each position is responsible for covering a specific area on the ice. The object of the game is to get the puck—a hard rubber disk—into the other team's net for a goal.

Unlike other sports, there are not always an equal number of players competing on each side. When a player gets a penalty, he or she has to spend a certain amount of time in the penalty box. That team then has one fewer player on the ice. This gives the other side an advantage, known as a power play. It improves their chances of scoring.

STEM ON THE ICE

The principles of STEM are in play during every hockey game. Science is behind the way energy is transferred from the player to the stick to the puck. Laws of physics determine how the puck moves across the ice, including what causes it to change speed and direction. Technology also plays a role in the sport. Game footage on tablet computers helps teams prepare for games by showing what their opponents are doing. In addition, sensors and cameras in players' equipment provide live feeds of data and video.

Hockey sticks have evolved from wood to composite materials that are lightweight and flexible. Engineering has led to more comfortable and advanced skates, helmets, and gear. Math is also a factor. It dictates the

Detroit Red Wings player Dylan Larkin wears a camera on his helmet during an All-Star Game skills competition.

angle the puck takes when it leaves the stick's blade. In addition, principles of mathematics are used to determine statistics, which help coaches and players form game plans. Players may not stop to think about STEM principles every time they make a big shot or thrilling save, but they are using these ideas every time they get on the ice.

Hard slap shots can noticeably bend the stick.

2

SCIENCE IN MOTION

One of the most exciting plays in hockey is the slap shot. Players get in position, swing the stick high over their heads, and then bring it down to hit the puck extremely hard. Players can send the puck flying at super-fast speeds. The fastest slap shot was recorded at 110.3 miles per hour (177.5 km/h).

Many factors come together in the slap shot. It's called "hockey's hardest shot" and is a perfect example of physics

on the ice. The stick hits the ice just behind the puck.
As it strikes the ice, the end of the stick bends back.
It stores potential energy. When the stick lifts off the
ice a fraction of a second later, it snaps back toward its
original shape. It turns the potential energy into kinetic
energy that is transferred to the puck.

PUCK CONTROL

Force, acceleration, and friction all come into play when
a player shoots the puck. The puck's motion follows
Sir Isaac Newton's laws of motion. Newton described his
three laws in the late 1600s.

His second law of motion dictates how the force of a
hockey stick sets the puck in motion. The law states that
force equals mass times acceleration. In hockey terms,
the force that goes into a shot can be calculated by
multiplying the mass of the puck by its acceleration off
the stick. The faster a player hits the puck, the faster it
moves, and the harder it is for the goalie to stop.

SWING

CONTACT WITH ICE

CONTACT WITH PUCK

MOTION OF PUCK

During the slap shot, the player rotates his body as he lifts the stick overhead for the windup. The player then swings the stick, bringing it crashing down. He shifts his weight from the back to the front skate. The stick briefly hits the ice before hitting the puck. This causes the stick to flex, giving it more energy. The momentum from the stick and the player is moved to the puck, sending it airborne.

Skilled players use the stick's blade to maintain control of the puck at high speeds.

The shape of the stick itself also allows players to control the puck. The bottom of the stick, where it contacts the puck, is called the blade. The blade is curved. This allows it to cradle the puck, giving the player more control. When the player takes a shot, the curve ensures the puck leaves from the same part of the blade every time. The blade curve also puts a spin on the puck, keeping it in a straight line during flight. Players apply tape on their blades to create more friction. This slows the puck's movement against the blade, allowing for better puck control.

THE MECHANICS OF SKATING

To accelerate, players dig their skate blades into the ice for traction as they lean forward. By leaning, players allow gravity to work to their advantage by pulling them forward.

The blade along the bottom of hockey skates is designed to give players the ability to quickly speed up, turn, and stop. The outside edges of the blade are slightly taller than the middle section. The middle is called the blade hollow. This results in two sharp edges that bite into the ice so players don't slip. The depth of the hollow varies depending on the preference of the individual player.

Friction between the blade and the ice melts the ice, creating a very thin film of water that acts as a lubricant. The more water on the blade, the faster a player can skate. Some NHL players can skate at more than 20 miles per hour (32 km/h).

FAST AND SLOW ICE

Not all ice is created equal. As hockey players know well, there is "fast ice" and "slow ice." Not all rinks freeze their ice at the same temperature. Fast ice is harder because it's colder and therefore smoother, which lets the players skate faster. Slow ice is softer and has a rougher surface. This slows down players and dulls their blades. Additionally, the rough surface makes puck handling more difficult. The puck is more likely to lift off the ice and change direction if the surface is bumpy. Between periods of a hockey game, a vehicle called an ice resurfacer is driven across the ice. It makes the ice smooth again. These vehicles are also known as Zambonis.

Pucks for the 2006 Winter Olympics sit in a freezer between games.

FREEZING THE PUCK

Pucks are made from hard, vulcanized rubber. Before games, each puck is frozen. This keeps it from bouncing. A frozen puck is more likely to remain flat on the ice than a warm puck, which can lift up, roll onto its side, or flip end over end. A puck that remains flat is easier to control. Each NHL team has a freezer in its locker room that stores at least 80 frozen game pucks.

Players study game footage on tablets before and even during games.

3

NEW TECH CHANGES THE GAME

Advances in technology have changed many aspects of hockey, including how it's coached. Like any competitive sport, hockey requires strategy. Before games, coaches and players watch videos to study their opponents. Coaches then form a game plan based on what they saw.

Professional teams use video during games to make adjustments.

Studying an opponent can give a player an edge during a thrilling shootout.

Coaches show replays on tablets to point out what the opposing team is doing. They can also use the tablets to draw up new plays and share them instantly with players. Each NHL team has three tablets on the bench to review plays, a policy that started in the 2017 playoffs.

If an NHL game is tied after the overtime period, the teams have a shootout. That means a player starts at mid-rink and goes one-on-one against the goalie, skating the puck toward the net to score. For fans, a shootout is one of the most exciting parts of the game. If a goalie makes a mistake, it could cost his team the game. To prepare for shootouts, goalies watch videos on tablets to see how skaters shoot the puck. This helps them prepare for each individual opponent.

SMART CLOTHING PROVIDES PLAYER INFORMATION

As the final seconds tick off the game clock, the center steals the puck. She skates it up the ice, taps the puck twice to get it under control, then fires off the shot. The puck sails over the top of the net, so she doesn't score. The player isn't sure what she did wrong. But she may be able to find out by looking at data collected by her equipment.

Some hockey gear has sensors inside that provide data about the player. The wearable technology tracks the athlete's heart rate, breathing, calories burned, body temperature, and other details. Wearables are being combined with wireless technology. This allows player data to be sent instantly to coaches. The data can also be shared with fans on television or in the arena.

TECHNOLOGY IN ACTION

KEEPING TRACK OF PLAYERS

The NHL uses player tracking technology. Sensors are placed in pucks and worn inside players' jerseys, providing a variety of data. The data includes puck and skating speed, puck trajectory, the distance skated by players, and the spacing between players. The data is collected 30 times per second. The information can be shown on broadcasts. This lets fans know, for example, how fast their favorite player was skating on a breakaway.

Today's skates are high-tech pieces of equipment designed for speed, agility, and comfort.

CUSTOM-FIT HOCKEY SKATES

Players used to buy skates the same way they bought shoes. They simply picked a pair that matched their foot size. More recently, players have used technology to "bake" their skates for a more precise fit. First the skate is heated in a special oven. Then the player sticks his foot inside and ties the skate tightly. After 15 minutes or so, the warm skate is molded to the shape of his foot. The latest technology allows another method of custom fitting. A 3-D body scan enables manufacturers to build the gear to match each player's exact body type.

The gear and skates are made from strong, lightweight materials. This allows players to skate fast and maintain agility on the ice while still being protected from hard hits. During the course of a game, this lighter equipment can make a big difference.

SEE WHAT PLAYERS SEE

Fans often wonder what it's like to be a pro hockey player. Now, with body cameras, they can get close to the real experience. Players and referees wear cameras to let fans see games from their perspectives. Fans can see every breakaway and big hit from the players' viewpoints. Goalies also wear cameras, so fans see what

INFRARED
LIGHTS

Not all experiments with new hockey technology have been successful. In 1996 the Fox television network introduced a technology it called FoxTrax. It added sensors and lights to the puck. The lights were invisible to the human eye, but a tracking system detected them. Computers followed the position of the puck and gave it a blue glow to make it easier to see on television. On hard shots, the puck would have a red glow. However, fans disliked FoxTrax. Many found it distracting. It was last used in 1998.

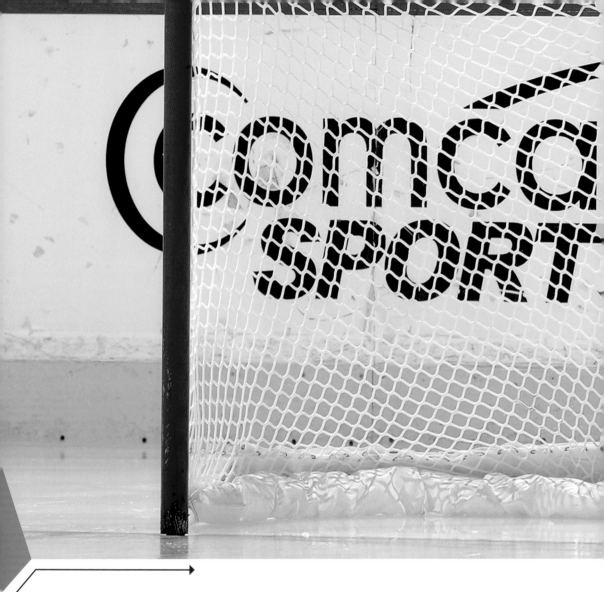

it's like to have a player charging the net on a breakaway or a puck flying at them at high speed.

The videos are used for broadcasts. The technology provides the type of in-your-face action that fans love. Fans also get the point of view of officials. Their cameras

Durable, protected cameras are placed in the backs of nets before NHL games.

show how they often have to make calls in just a split second. Officials might also gain some sympathy thanks to the cameras. Their footage often shows players yelling at them during games.

The hockey sticks and gear of the 1930s were significantly different from the modern versions created by advanced engineering.

4

ENGINEERING HOCKEY

Engineering has led to many improvements in hockey sticks and gear. From the mid-1800s to the mid-1900s, hockey sticks were made of wood. In the 1950s, fiberglass was added for reinforcement. Today's sticks are made of composites. Composites are made of two or more other materials. They are often light, strong, and relatively inexpensive.

The first composite stick, called the Synergy, came out in 1999. It weighed 30 percent less than wooden sticks, but it was

HEEL

LIMIT:
0.75 INCHES
(1.9 CM)

The blade of a hockey stick has a curve. This forms a space where the player can easily cradle the puck while skating. The result is improved puck control. However, the NHL sets limits to a stick's curve. An imaginary line is drawn from the tip of the blade to its base. An imaginary line from this line down to the bottom of the curve cannot be longer than 0.75 inches (1.9 cm). The NHL sets this limit to avoid making it too easy for players to keep control of the puck. Deeper curves also lead to shots that go higher in the air. Limiting the curve keeps shots closer to the ice, improving safety.

just as strong. By 2004, about 90 percent of NHL players were using sticks made with composite technology. Today, almost every player relies on a composite stick. These sticks are either a mixture of carbon fiber and fiberglass, or they are all carbon fiber. The sticks bend, or flex, more than wood, allowing players to shoot the puck harder. Because the sticks are lightweight, players can swing faster than ever, giving goalies less time to react.

Today NHL players get their sticks custom-made. This ensures the stick has the precise qualities each player wants, from the curve of the blade to the length of the handle to the amount of flex and the angle of the blade to the handle.

THE QUEST FOR THE PERFECT SKATE

Companies continue to improve skates. A recent model has a spring-loaded blade, increasing speed while also reducing stress on the body. When the skate touches the ice, a spring absorbs the energy that would otherwise transfer up the body to the knee joint. As the player pushes off the ice, the spring moves, pushing the player forward. Removing stress helps reduce injuries and could extend players' careers.

PROTECTING THE HEAD

Concussions are brain injuries caused by blows to the head. They are a problem at every level of hockey, from youth through the pros. Helmets have improved to reduce the risk of head injuries. Engineers have designed

WHY THE STINK?

As anyone who's ever played or been around the sport of hockey knows, the gear can smell foul after a practice or game. Players sweat heavily in it. Continued wear and more sweat lets bacteria thrive, causing a strong smell. Airing out or washing gear usually isn't enough to tame the odor, and sprays mask the stench without eliminating the source. The bacteria, mold, and mildew have to be removed to get rid of the stink. New deodorizers are being engineered to kill the bacteria, which then eliminates the smell. One such product is used on a player's hands to get rid of the smell left by sweaty gloves.

Goalies are protected by large, sturdy helmets.

smart helmets with sensors that measure the force and location of impact. The sensors send an alert to coaches through a smartphone app that tells them if a player has a possible concussion. This keeps the player from staying in a game and risking further injury.

Sensor kits are also available that attach to any sports helmet. The sensor sends data to a smartphone or tablet through a wireless transmission. The sensor counts how many times a player is hit and measures the force of those hits.

PROTECTING TEETH

Hockey players used to be notorious for their missing teeth. Pucks would hit them in the face and cause severe damage. They wore little protective gear. That's changed in the modern era. Players now wear mouth guards to protect their teeth. The latest generation of mouth guards is engineered to monitor concussions, too. One has sensors that measure the impact of a hit and determine the likelihood of a concussion. If the player sustains that type of a collision, the mouth guard lights up. At the same time, data is sent to a smartphone or tablet app to alert coaches about the possibility of an injury.

Columbus Blue Jackets player Jack Johnson adjusts his mouth guard.

Each time a player shoots the puck, he or she is
taking angles into account.

5

MATH ON ICE

Math is always in play in hockey. Players are constantly thinking about angles for shots on goal, while goalies are getting in the best position to stop the shots. A player has a larger target if the goalie stays close to the net, leaving more room on either side of the goalie to score. When goalies come away from the net, they cut off some angles for a shot, but they also take themselves out of position for other angles.

Every player who straps on a pair of skates hears the famous quote from hockey legend Wayne Gretzky: "I skate to where the puck is going to be, not where it has been." This explains how he uses math. If a player skates to where he sees the puck, by the time he gets there, even if it only takes a couple of seconds, the puck will have moved. Smart players like Gretzky study the puck's speed, their own speed, and the direction the puck is traveling. Then they attack the puck at an angle to intercept it.

PLAYING THE ANGLES

A hockey rink is surrounded by wooden boards that make up its border. The boards are often called the "seventh teammate" because players hit the puck off them to make passes.

Math, especially geometry, allows players to make accurate passes. When a puck hits the boards, the angle of incidence is equal to the angle of reflection. This means the puck will come off the boards at the same

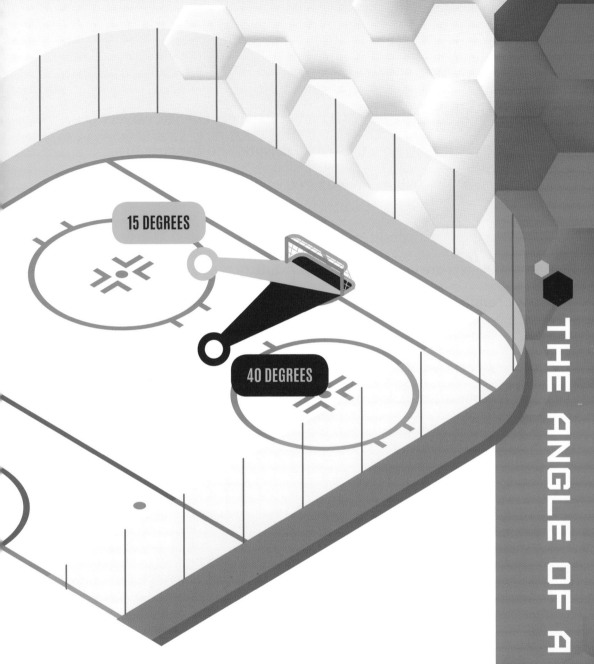

15 DEGREES

40 DEGREES

A player's position on the ice determines the angle needed to shoot the puck on target. Players facing the net head-on have the widest angle to shoot at. If they are skating off to the side, their angle narrows and they must be more accurate with their shots to have a chance at scoring.

angle it hit the boards. From years of experience, players know exactly how these angles work, and they use the angles to their advantage every time they're in the rink.

A GAME OF NUMBERS

Players are compared by their statistics, such as goals and assists. The stats do more than feed debates about who the best players are. Coaches know which opposing players are statistically most likely to score and which types of shots are more successful against specific goalies. Jim Corsi, a former NHL goaltending coach, went

WHERE FANTASY AND REALITY MEET

Joining a fantasy league and building a fantasy team have become popular across major sports. Fans build a team of real players, and then they get points based on how their players perform on game day. This lets fans pick their favorite hockey players for each position, creating a "fantasy" team. Passionate fantasy players study statistics to pick their team and trade players throughout the season. They try to determine which players are most likely to rack up points and help their fantasy team win.

so far as to create his own formula for figuring out stats for shots depending on which players are on the ice.

A player's Corsi rating shows how many shots on goal were made by his team and against his team when he was on the ice. This lets teams know which players are most likely to shoot the puck, allowing them to form strategies to cover those players.

LAWS OF PROBABILITIES

By analyzing game data, teams know probabilities. Probabilities use math to show what factors are common in games won and lost. For example, the team that scores first has a better chance of winning. According to the math, the team that scores the first goal wins 67 percent of the time.

At the start of the season, every team wants to win enough games to make the playoffs. Throughout the season, teams are ranked by their number of wins. Each team has a certain probability of winning enough games to advance to the playoffs.

At some point, teams are mathematically eliminated. This means that no matter how many games they win for the rest of the season, they cannot make the playoffs. Other teams win enough games in the regular season that they are guaranteed a playoff spot.

Hockey is one of the most thrilling games to play and watch. It features nonstop action, fast skaters, and flying pucks. Understanding the STEM principles behind these elements of hockey adds another level of excitement to the sport.

Keeping track of data, probabilities, and statistics can help a team as it fights to win the Stanley Cup.

GLOSSARY

ACCELERATE
To change in speed or direction.

COMPOSITE
Made up of different materials.

CONCUSSION
An injury to the brain caused by a violent collision.

KINETIC ENERGY
The energy of moving objects.

LUBRICANT
A substance that helps objects slide across each other more smoothly.

PROBABILITY
The branch of mathematics that studies the likelihood that events will occur.

SENSOR
A device that detects things such as movement, light, or heat.

TRAJECTORY
The path an object takes as it moves.

VULCANIZE
To treat rubber with chemicals to give it useful properties, such as strength and stability.

WIRELESS
Able to transmit data through the air, without wires.

ONLINE RESOURCES

Booklinks
NONFICTION NETWORK
FREE! ONLINE NONFICTION RESOURCES

To learn more about STEM in hockey, visit
abdobooklinks.com. These links are routinely monitored and
updated to provide the most current information available.

MORE INFORMATION

BOOKS

Haché, Alain. *Slap Shot Science: A Curious Fan's Guide to
Hockey*. Baltimore, MD: John Hopkins University Press,
2015.

Slingerland, Janet. *Sports Science and Technology in the Real
World*. Minneapolis, MN: Abdo Publishing, 2017.

Vizard, Frank. *Why a Curveball Curves: The Incredible Science of
Sports*. New York: Hearst Books, 2014.

INDEX

ABOUT THE AUTHOR

Brett S. Martin has more than 20 years of writing experience. He has written several fiction and nonfiction books. He has also volunteered as a youth football coach for nine seasons. Martin lives in Shakopee, Minnesota, with his wife and two teenage sons.